IN THEIR OWN WORDS

ABRAHAM LINCOLN

George Sullivan

SCHOLASTIC
REFERENCE

ACKNOWLEDGMENTS

Many people helped me in providing helpful background information and illustrations for use in this book. Several reviewed all or portions of the manuscript for accuracy. I'm grateful to each of these individuals. Special thanks are due Dan Pearson, Lincoln Fellowship of Wisconsin; Cindy Van Horn, the Lincoln Museum; Maja Keech, Division of Prints and Photographs, Library of Congress; Heather Egan, National Portrait Gallery; Jean Ashton, Columbia University; Sal Alberti and James Lowe, James Lowe Autographs; Kim Bauer, Illinois State Historical Library; James T. Parker II, Archival Research International; Jonathan Mann, *The Rail Splitter*; Ellen LiBretto, Ballantine Books, Lois Wimsett, Abraham Lincoln's Boyhood Home; Norman D. Hellmers, Lincoln Home National Historic Site; Dusty Schultz, Lincoln Boyhood National Memorial; Kim Rosendahl, Springfield Visitors Bureau; and Lloyd Ostendorf and Don Wigal.

GEORGE SULLIVAN
NEW YORK CITY

Sullivan, George, 1927–

Abraham Lincoln / by George Sullivan

p. cm.—(In their own words)

Includes bibliographical references and index.

Summary: Presents a biography, including excerpts from his speeches, letters, and other writings, of the man who was president during the Civil War.

ISBN 0-439-09554-9

1. Lincoln, Abraham, 1809–1865 Juvenile literature. 2. Presidents—United States Biography Juvenile literature. [1. Lincoln, Abraham, 1809–1865. 2. Presidents.] I. Title. II. Series: In their own words (Scholastic)

E457.905.S85 2000   973.7'092—dc21   99-33387   [B]   CIP

10 9 8 7 6 5 4   0/0   01   02   03

Composition by Brad Walrod

Printed in the U.S.A.   40

First printing, January 2000

CONTENTS

INTRODUCTION

"FOUR SCORE AND SEVEN YEARS AGO, our fathers brought forth on this continent a new nation, conceived in liberty, and dedicated to the proposition that all men are created equal."

These are the opening words of Abraham Lincoln's Gettysburg Address. Only ten sentences long, it is often called the most famous speech in American history.

At the time Lincoln gave the speech, the Civil War was raging. Lincoln began by reminding people of the nation's beginnings. He noted that the founding fathers had created the "new nation" in 1776. It was based, he said, on the idea that all citizens have an equal right to freedom.

He used the speech to stir people of the North. He urged them to continue the struggle to save the nation.

Abraham Lincoln was the sixteenth president of the United States. His words and deeds have made him a towering figure in American history.

Lincoln helped keep America from breaking apart in its greatest crisis, the Civil War. He helped put an end to slavery.

Abraham Lincoln understood the power of words. He used simple language to express great ideas. He used

Mrs. Lincoln called this "the best likeness she had ever seen" of her husband. It was made in Chicago on October 4, 1859.

words to influence people. He used words to lead them.

Lincoln's speeches and letters help us to answer questions about him. These documents are primary sources.

Primary sources are actual records that have been handed down from the past. Speeches and letters aren't the only primary sources. So are diaries, maps, and government documents.

Notes to a friend or e-mail messages are primary sources.

A picture of your mother is a primary source.

Secondary sources are descriptions written by people about events some time after they happened. Your history textbook is a secondary source. An encyclopedia is a secondary source. So is this biography of Lincoln.

Serious students use primary sources in writing reports and biographies. (Books that contain Lincoln's speeches, letters, and other writings are listed at the back of this book.)

In working with a primary source, try to understand its meaning. When was it written? Where was it written? Why was it written? What audience was being addressed? What was the speaker seeking to accomplish?

Some primary sources give clues to Lincoln's character. From them, one can get an understanding of what he was thinking, feeling, and hoping.

His speech at Gettysburg is one example of this. Lincoln felt that if the American nation were to split apart it would be a great tragedy. It would be taken as evidence that people were not able to govern themselves. It would be a severe blow to democracy everywhere.

In the final sentences of his Gettysburg Address, Lincoln sought to communicate this idea. He called "for us to be here dedicated to the great task remaining before us...that these dead shall not have died in vain; that this nation, under God, shall have a new birth of freedom—and that government of the people, by the people, for the people, shall not perish from the earth."

CHAPTER 2

YOUNG ABE LINCOLN

"IF ANY PERSONAL DESCRIPTION OF ME is thought desirable, it may be said, I am, in height, six feet four inches, nearly; lean in flesh, weighing on an average, one hundred and eighty pounds; dark complexion, with coarse black hair and grey eyes—no other marks or brands recollected."

Late in December 1859, Lincoln wrote a brief history of his life for a friend. It was to be used as part of a newspaper article. The paragraph above is from that sketch.

"I was born Feb. 12, 1809, in Hardin County, Kentucky," the sketch says. "My parents were both born in Virginia..."

Abraham Lincoln's father was named Thomas Lincoln. He lived a hard life as a farmer. In 1806, when he was twenty-eight, Thomas Lincoln married Nancy Hanks. Little is known of her.

After their marriage, Tom and Nancy built a log cabin in Elizabethtown, Kentucky. Their first child, a daughter named Sarah, was born in 1807.

Not long after Sarah's birth, the family moved. Thomas Lincoln bought a farm at nearby Sinking Spring in Hardin County.

The Lincolns built a log cabin on the property. It had one door that opened and closed on leather hinges. It had a packed-dirt floor.

The cabin was tiny. It had only one room.

It was here that Abraham Lincoln was born on February 12, 1809. Today, Abraham Lincoln's birthplace is often given as Hodgenville.

Thomas Lincoln was a restless man. The Lincolns lived only two years on the farm where Abraham was born. They moved on to Knob Creek, Kentucky, about ten miles away. There Thomas Lincoln built a new cabin. It, too, had but one room.

This one-room log cabin in Hardin County, Kentucky, was Lincoln's home as an infant. It was built by his father.

Because the Lincolns lived in a log cabin, many people think the family was poverty-stricken. They believe that Lincoln's boyhood was harsh. But at that time, eighty to ninety percent of the white population lived in one-room houses.

The Lincolns were not poor. The family was as well-fed and as well-clothed as other families.

Lincoln long held memories of what he called "the Knob Creek place." It was surrounded, he recalled, by "high hills" and "deep gorges."

Flowing near the Lincolns' cabin was a creek that gave the place its name. Young Abe once fell into its waters. A boy who lived nearby waded in to rescue him.

During his years in Kentucky, Thomas Lincoln had trouble over the legal rights to his property. These problems drove him to move again. This time he decided to leave Kentucky and head west to Indiana. There people could buy land directly from the government.

Abraham Lincoln was seven at the time. He never forgot the harsh journey to the new home.

It began on a bitter, cold day in 1816. The family loaded their few possessions on horseback. They then set out for the Ohio River. At what is now Cloverport, Kentucky, they crossed the river by ferry into Indiana.

Once in Indiana, they plunged into thick forests in the southwestern part of the state. Often they had to hack their way through thick underbrush.

When they arrived at their property, it was cold and wintry. They quickly built a crude shelter. Made of logs, it had three sides. The fourth side was a fireplace. It had to be fed logs day and night.

Early the next year, Thomas Lincoln built a log cabin. Abraham helped. The site was just south of Little Pigeon Creek. It is now Lincoln City, Indiana.

Abraham Lincoln never thought fondly of the place. Life was harder there than it had ever been in Kentucky.

Once the cabin

This is the only known photograph of Thomas Lincoln, Abraham Lincoln's father.

was built, there was much work to be done. Trees had to be cut. The land had to be cleared of rocks, brush, and tree stumps. Only then could Thomas Lincoln begin farming.

Young Abraham once described the role he played: "The clearing away of surplus wood was the great task ahead," he wrote. "Abraham, though still very young, was large for his age, and had an axe put in his hands at once; and from that till within his twenty-third year, he was almost constantly handling that most useful instrument—less, of course, in plowing and harvesting seasons."

Not long after the Lincolns moved to Little Pigeon Creek, Thomas and Elizabeth Sparrow joined them. They were relatives of Nancy's. With them came a boy named Dennis Hanks. Dennis was nineteen. Although Dennis was almost ten years older than Abraham, he became young Abe's best friend.

Late in the summer of 1818, a terrible disease known as milk sickness swept across southwestern Indiana. It was caused by poison in the milk of cows.

It resulted when the cows ate a poisonous plant called white snakeroot.

Lincoln's mother died from the disease. So did Thomas and Elizabeth Sparrow.

Nine-year-old Abraham helped to make his mother's coffin. She was buried on a hill not far from their cabin.

The winter that followed was a sad and lonely time for the Lincoln children. Sarah, twelve years old, took over for her mother. She cooked and cleaned and sewed and mended.

The next winter, Thomas Lincoln went back to Elizabethtown. He was gone for two months. When he returned, he brought a new wife with him. She was a widow named Sarah Bush Johnston. She had three children, ages five, eight, and twelve.

The expanded family crowded into the one-room cabin. All traces of loneliness disappeared.

Sarah and Abraham found their new stepmother to be a loving and fair-minded woman. She raised her two stepchildren as her own. She was especially fond of Abraham. He once described her as "my angel mother."

Thomas Lincoln brought up his son to be a farmer like himself. Young Abraham plowed the fields. He planted seeds. He fed the animals. At harvesttime, he cut corn.

And young Lincoln split logs into rails. Farmers needed wooden rails for making fences. Rail fences kept the farmers' cows and pigs from getting loose.

Young Abraham never liked farmwork. Some people said that he was lazy. But others recalled that he was a "hard and faithful worker."

Abe had his own thoughts on the subject. "My

Sarah Bush Lincoln, the stepmother of Abraham Lincoln. This engraving is based on a photograph of her that was taken in 1865.

father taught me to work," he said. "But he never taught me to like it."

Between spring plowing and fall harvesting, Lincoln sometimes got in some schooling. He went to school "by littles," he once said. He meant a little now, a little then. All of his schooling totaled no more than one year.

Books and paper were scarce on the frontier. Lincoln's stepmother once recalled how he used to work out arithmetic problems at home. He would write each one down in charcoal upon a wooden board. Once finished, he would scrape the board clean with a knife for the next problem.

Lincoln later received a "sum book" of blank pages. In this he wrote some playful lines of poetry. Here are some samples:

Abraham Lincoln, his hand and pen,
He will be good, but God knows when.

Abraham Lincoln is my nam[e]
And with my pen I wrote the same.

I wrote in both hast[e] and speed
And left it here for fools to read.

Lincoln loved to read. But books were scarce on the frontier. Lincoln would walk a long way to borrow a book.

History and biography interested him the most. *Aesop's Fables, Robinson Crusoe, Pilgrim's Progress,* Grimshaw's *History of the United States,* and the Bible were among the books that he enjoyed reading.

Lincoln liked to read at night in his loft bed. One night he was reading a book that he had borrowed from a neighbor. The book was a biography of George Washington. He read until his candle went out. Then he stuck the book in the wall in an opening between two logs. That night it rained. The book got soaked.

Abraham didn't have the money to pay for the book. He worked on the neighbor's farm to repay the book's cost.

Through most of his teenage years, Lincoln kept busy clearing land and farming. Sometimes when chores were done for the day, he and Dennis Hanks would walk over to Gentryville. The village was about a mile and a half from the Lincoln cabin. At the Gentryville general store, he and Dennis and other farm boys would sit around and swap stories and jokes. Lincoln enjoyed these get-togethers. He became a skilled storyteller.

When he was seventeen, Abe's sister, Sarah, married and moved away. (Sarah was to die in childbirth a year and a half later.)

Besides farming and clearing land, Abe did other work. None of it was easy. He split rails for fences, of course. He cut firewood. He killed hogs and helped out on a ferryboat.

In his spare time, Abe built a small rowboat. Two men asked him to row them out into the river where their steamer was at anchor. When they went aboard, each of them tossed a silver half-dollar to Abe as payment. That was quite a bit of money for a young boy in those days.

Abe gasped in amazement. "I could scarcely believe my eyes as I picked up the money," Lincoln

Lincoln, as a rail-splitter, wields a maul, a heavy hammer with a wooden head used for driving a wedge.

was later to recall. "I...a poor boy, had earned a dollar in less than a day. The world seemed wider and fairer before me."

Later that same year, Lincoln took part in a bold adventure. He and a friend named Allen Gentry took a cargo of meat, corn, and flour to New Orleans by way of the Ohio and Mississippi rivers. During the day, they used long poles to push the boat along with the current. They tied up the boat along the banks of the Mississippi at night. When they reached New Orleans, they sold their cargo. They also sold their boat. They returned home by river steamer.

The journey was a voyage of discovery for young Lincoln. It opened his eyes to the world beyond Little Pigeon Creek.

CHAPTER 3

NEW SALEM YEARS

IN MARCH 1830, THOMAS LINCOLN uprooted his family again. He was not doing badly in Indiana. But he had been hearing stories of the wonders of Illinois, of the rich, black soil there. He moved the family to a farm about ten miles west of Decatur.

Abraham was twenty-one now. He was six feet four inches tall. He was muscular and very strong.

After the family moved to Illinois, Abraham helped his father build their log cabin home. He helped clear the land. And he split the rails for the farm's fences.

The next spring Lincoln left home to set out for himself. A trader named Denton Offutt hired Lincoln and two other young men to build him

This typical split-rail fence stands not far from the reconstructed village of New Salem.

an eighty-foot flatboat. They then took the boat and a load of cargo to New Orleans.

When they returned from New Orleans, Offutt offered Lincoln a job. Offutt planned to open a general store in New Salem, a village on the Sangamon River northwest of Springfield. He asked Lincoln to work as a manager in the store.

Lincoln was happy to accept the offer. The job meant an end to land clearing and wood splitting. He would get to use his head a little.

Lincoln lived in New Salem for almost six years.

It was a rowdy frontier village. About a hundred people lived there.

As manager of Offutt's store, Lincoln joked and swapped stories with customers. On his days off, he took part in footraces and wrestling matches.

Denton Offutt boasted that Lincoln was the best wrestler in New Salem. That led to a challenge from Jack Armstrong, the town's wrestling champion. Armstrong was also leader of a local gang known as the Clary Grove Boys.

On the day of the match, practically the whole town gathered to watch. Both men stripped to the waist. They grunted and grabbed for about half an hour. Then Lincoln came close to pinning Armstrong to the ground. Members of the Clary Grove Boys swarmed into the brawl. They separated the two men and flung Lincoln back against a wall. Lincoln was unafraid. He dared the whole gang to fight him—one at a time.

Armstrong himself came forward to act as peacemaker. He held out his hand to Lincoln. The match, he declared, should be called a draw.

Lincoln became very popular with the Clary Grove Boys after that. They admired him for his physical strength. They enjoyed him as a storyteller. And they were impressed by his honesty. Lincoln always told the truth.

Lincoln liked being friends with the Clary Grove Boys. But he also sought out members of the town who could help him improve his mind. The local schoolmaster lent Lincoln history books. A local judge encouraged Lincoln to start writing contracts and other legal documents. The future president joined the New Salem Debating Society to improve his skills as a public speaker.

Lincoln had plenty of time to read at Offutt's store because there weren't many customers. Offutt closed the store in 1832. Lincoln was out of a job.

Politics had always interested Lincoln. As a clerk in Offutt's store, he had spent countless hours in discussing political affairs. Lincoln now decided to run for public office. He announced that he would be a candidate for the Illinois Legislature. The legislature made the laws for the state. Lincoln's many friends promised him their support.

But before Lincoln had much of a chance to campaign, Chief Black Hawk's War began. The war had its beginnings when the federal government forced the Native-American Sauk and Fox nations out of Illinois across the Mississippi River into Iowa. But they were unable to find food there. Black Hawk then led a band of Sauk and Fox back into Illinois. They were looking for food. They also hoped to regain their land.

Fighting broke out. The governor of Illinois called for volunteers for the citizens' army, the militia. Lincoln volunteered. The men in his unit voted him their captain.

Lincoln and his men were sent to northern Illinois. He and his men saw no Sauk and Fox there.

Other troops drove Black Hawk north into Wisconsin. Many of Black Hawk's warriors were massacred trying to recross the Mississippi back to Iowa. So ended Black Hawk's War.

By the time Lincoln got back to New Salem, the

election was only two weeks away. He plunged into the campaign. He chatted with customers at country stores. He spoke with farmers in their fields. He mounted tree stumps or boxes to give short speeches.

Despite his efforts, Lincoln lost the election. He was disappointed. But he had enjoyed the experience. Politics and campaigning excited him. He looked forward to 1834 and the chance to run again.

He needed something to do in the meantime. When the chance came for him and a partner to buy a country store in New Salem, he jumped at it. But Lincoln was no businessman. The store soon failed. Lincoln said that he and his partner "did nothing but get deeper and deeper into debt."

Lincoln took odd jobs to help pay back the money that he owed. He even worked as a farmhand. Years went by before Lincoln was able to wipe out his debts.

In 1833, Lincoln was named postmaster of New Salem. He also was offered a chance to work with the county surveyor. He borrowed books on the

A re-created version of the general store owned by Lincoln and a partner. The store failed.

subject and studied hard. He also borrowed the money he needed to buy surveying instruments. Before long, Lincoln was traveling through the county to lay out roads and town sites.

In 1834, Lincoln ran for the state legislature a second time. He ran as a Whig. The Whigs were a political party that wanted more roads and waterways for Illinois. This time Lincoln was successful.

At the age of twenty-five, Lincoln was starting a

new career. He bought a tailor-made suit. It was the first suit he had ever owned. It cost him sixty dollars. He boarded a stagecoach for the ride to Vandalia, then the state capital.

Among the other election winners that fall was a young lawyer from Springfield named John Todd Stuart. He had already served a term in the legislature.

Stuart urged Lincoln to become a lawyer. Being a lawyer was the surest way to become successful in politics, Stuart told him. Lincoln had thought of becoming a lawyer. But he had dismissed the idea because of his lack of education.

Lincoln now noted that many of the lawyers in the state legislature had never attended college. Each had simply "read law" in the office of an attorney. Lincoln borrowed law books and began to study.

Years later, Lincoln gave advice to a young man who wanted to become a lawyer. What he said reveals what he must have been thinking in 1835. "If you are resolutely determined to make a lawyer of yourself, the thing is more than half done already,"

Lincoln said. "Get the books and read and study them. . . .

"Always bear in mind that your own resolution to succeed, is more important than any one thing."

In the summer of 1835, Lincoln was brought depressing news. A pretty New Salem girl named Ann Rutledge had died of "brain fever." Lincoln was deeply saddened.

Some sources say that Lincoln and Ann Rutledge were in love and planned to marry. Many historians believe they were merely good friends.

The next year, Lincoln met Mary Owens. From Kentucky, she had come to New Salem to visit relatives. She was smart. She was from a good family. Lincoln liked her. When he eventually proposed marriage, she turned him down.

Lincoln later laughed about the romance. He said that he had "made a fool" of himself.

"I have now come to the conclusion never again to think of marrying; and for this reason: I can never be satisfied with any one who would be block-head enough to have me."

CHAPTER 4

LINCOLN THE LAWYER

O N SEPTEMBER 9, 1836, LINCOLN achieved his goal. He received a license to practice law in the state of Illinois.

Lincoln then accepted an offer to become a junior partner in John Todd Stuart's law firm in Springfield. He went back to New Salem for the last time in April 1837. He packed his belongings in two big saddlebags and said good-bye to his friends.

Springfield at the time was a frontier town of about 1,500 people. Hogs rooted in the muddy streets. In summer, the dust was choking. Prairie fires at night would sometimes light the sky and rain ashes on the community.

Lincoln moved to Springfield, Illinois, in 1837 and became a partner in a law firm there. This is a view of downtown Springfield in the 1850s.

The firm of Stuart & Lincoln prospered. Like other law firms of the day, their practice was not limited to Springfield.

The state of Illinois was divided into circuits. Each circuit was made up of several counties. Courts were established in each county. Most lawyers, and judges, too, would travel from one county to another for court sessions. This was known as "riding the circuit." On his favorite horse, "Old Tom," Lincoln rode regularly to McLean, Tazewell,

Macon, and Morgan counties. All are in central Illinois.

At the same time, Lincoln was becoming a leading figure among the Whigs in the state legislature. He was a gifted speaker. He was quick and bright as a debater.

Lincoln was reelected to the state legislature in 1838. In all, he would serve four terms.

Lincoln was very popular among the working men who supported him at election time. He liked being "one of the boys." He also sought friendships among the more well-to-do and influential citizens of Springfield, which had become the state capital in 1839.

So it was that Lincoln sometimes visited the mansion of Ninian and Elizabeth Edwards. They were one of Springfield's most fashionable couples.

There Lincoln met Mary Ann Todd. She was the daughter of a wealthy Kentucky merchant and banker.

Mary Todd lived with the Edwards family. Elizabeth Edwards was her older sister.

Lincoln never felt comfortable around women. He didn't know how to behave. This was partly because he had little or no chance to meet them. After he had been in Springfield for a month, he wrote, "I have been spoken to by but one woman since I've been here, and should not have been by her, if she could have avoided it."

But Lincoln felt at ease with the brown-haired, blue-eyed Mary Todd. She could be sweet and charming.

Lincoln didn't have to try to make conversation with her. Mary Todd always had something to say.

The two had many interests in common. Both were from Kentucky. Both loved poetry. They had even memorized some of the same poems. Both were interested in politics. Like Lincoln, Mary Todd was a Whig.

Lincoln was captivated by Mary. And Mary was fond of him. She liked his gentleness, good humor, and sense of fairness.

The two eventually married. The small wedding took place at the Edwards' home on November 4,

1842. Lincoln was thirty-three. His bride was ten years younger. He towered over her. On her finger he placed a ring that was engraved *Love is eternal*.

After the wedding, the couple moved into the Globe Tavern, a Springfield boardinghouse. There Lincoln rented a room for $4 a week.

On August 1, 1843, the Lincolns' first son was born. They named him Robert Todd Lincoln, after Mary's father.

Mary found life difficult. She was used to luxury and having servants. She had no training in keeping house, fixing meals, or caring for an infant.

This first-ever photograph of Mary Lincoln was also made in 1846. At the time, the Lincolns had been married for four years.

Lincoln, meanwhile, was making a success of his law career. He was earning from $1,200 to $1,500 a year. This was a better-than-average income for the time.

But in order to earn good money, Lincoln had to ride the circuit. Sometimes he was away as many as three months or more at a time. Mary didn't like being alone.

Things got better for Mary in 1844 when the Lincolns bought a large wood-frame home in Springfield. It had a tree-shaded lot and a small stable. The Lincolns' second son, Edward, was born there in 1846.

Lincoln continued to make his mark as a lawyer. After his partnership with John Todd Stuart and, later, Stephen T. Logan, had ended, Lincoln opened his own law firm. He then asked William H. Herndon to become his partner. Herndon was nine years younger than Lincoln. He had just received his license to practice law. Lincoln called him "Billy." To Herndon, however, his senior partner was always "Mr. Lincoln."

Abraham Lincoln spent the years from 1844 to 1861 in this house in Springfield. It is the only home he ever owned. It is now a National Historic Site, open to visitors.

Some people were surprised that Lincoln had chosen so young a lawyer for his partner. Lincoln knew what he was doing. One of Lincoln's failings was that he was careless as a record keeper. But Herndon, Lincoln said, "had a system to keep things in order."

Lincoln and Herndon had a long and very successful partnership. This was true despite the fact that young Herndon proved to be about as messy as

Lincoln was. Papers and documents were heaped on desks and tables. They were stuffed in drawers and crammed into boxes. The partners were always losing things.

Amid the clutter on his desk, Lincoln kept a bundle of papers with a string around it. A note on the bundle said, *When you can't find it anywhere else, look into this.*

Neither Lincoln nor Herndon ever sought another law partner. Some sixteen years after the firm was founded, Lincoln visited his old office before leaving Springfield to be sworn in as president. He happened to notice the signboard at the foot of the stairs. It bore the names of the two partners. "Let it hang there undisturbed," Lincoln said. "Give our clients to understand that the election of a President makes no change in the firm of Lincoln & Herndon."

A SEAT IN CONGRESS

AFTER HIS FOUR TERMS IN THE STATE legislature, Lincoln wanted a change. He wanted new worlds to conquer. He decided that he would seek election to the U.S. House of Representatives. In the election in the fall of 1846, Lincoln was successful.

With the victory, the Lincolns packed up and moved to Washington. The family rented rooms in a boardinghouse just east of the Capitol.

Washington was the biggest city the Lincolns had ever seen. About 40,000 people lived there. The population included 2,000 slaves and 8,000 free African Americans.

Mary Lincoln got little pleasure from her life

This is the first photographic likeness of Abraham Lincoln. It was made in 1846. Lincoln is wearing his best suit, a starched shirt, and a carefully knotted black tie.

in Washington. She didn't like living in a boardinghouse again. It reminded her of those terrible days at the Globe Tavern. She had few friends in Washington and seldom left her room.

After three months, Mary Lincoln could put up with it no longer. She packed up and went back to her family in Kentucky. She took the children with her.

Lincoln was left alone. His work as a congressman kept him busy.

The nation's war with Mexico was the major issue of the day. The war had broken out in 1846. President James K. Polk claimed that Mexico had started the war. Mexicans had fired upon American soldiers on American soil, he said.

This wasn't true, Lincoln declared. He said that Polk and his fellow Democrats had gotten the country into the war. Their goal was to seize Mexican territory for the United States. Lincoln called the president "a miserably perplexed man."

Lincoln spoke out against the president for not ending the war. Then Mexico signed a peace treaty. Under its terms, the United States got land from Mexico that became the present states of California, Nevada, and Utah, most of Arizona and New Mexico, and parts of Wyoming and Colorado.

The nation cheered. President Polk was a hero.

The Mexican War began in 1846. General Winfield Scott became a hero during the war. Above, the general enters Mexico City after capturing the city in September 1847.

Back home in Illinois, people questioned Lincoln and his antiwar stand. Even Billy Herndon thought that Polk had acted properly. Lincoln's popularity nose-dived.

President Polk did not seek to be reelected. An election to choose a new president was held in the fall of 1848.

That fall, Lincoln campaigned for General Zachary Taylor, the Whig candidate. Taylor had become a hero during the Mexican War.

Lincoln's travels on Taylor's behalf took him into New England. In Boston, Lincoln shared the speaker's platform with William H. Seward, the former governor of New York.

In his speech, Seward discussed the issue of slavery. Seward strongly opposed slavery.

The practice of keeping slaves in the American colonies began in the 1600s. Slavery had grown rapidly in the South. Big plantations there required large numbers of slaves to raise cotton, tobacco, and other crops. Few people in the North owned slaves, and opposition to slavery developed there.

After Seward had spoken, Lincoln went up to him. "Governor, I've been thinking about what you said in your speech," Lincoln said. "I reckon you are right. We have got to deal with this slavery question, and got to give much more attention to it hereafter than we have been doing."

Lincoln had earlier taken a stand on slavery. He had declared that "he ever was, on principle and in feeling, opposed to slavery."

As a congressman, Lincoln tried to introduce a bill to abolish slavery in the District of Columbia. But when the measure attracted opposition, Lincoln withdrew it.

There was a growing antislavery movement in Congress. But Lincoln played no active role in it.

After Congress ended its session, Lincoln returned to Springfield. He had campaigned with great energy for Zachary Taylor, who had been elected president. Lincoln ex-

General Zachary Taylor was another hero of the Mexican War. When he ran for president, Lincoln campaigned hard for him. Taylor became the twelfth U.S. president in 1849.

pected to be repaid in some way. Perhaps he would be given a rewarding job.

After a long wait, Lincoln finally received a job offer. He was asked whether he would like to serve as governor of the Oregon Territory. Lincoln thought about it. Mary didn't have to do any thinking. Oregon? She had no wish to live in the wilds of the Pacific Northwest. Lincoln turned down the offer.

Lincoln settled down in Springfield. He began again his career as a lawyer. He was forty years old now. His public career appeared to be over.

TURNING POINT

LINCOLN LOST INTEREST IN POLITICS for a time. He put all of his energy into his work as a lawyer.

On a typical day, Lincoln would awaken at dawn. He would go outside to feed and groom his horse. He would cut firewood.

It was about eight o'clock by the time he finished his chores. He would then have breakfast with Mary and the two boys. He might have an egg and some fruit. Lincoln always ate lightly.

After breakfast, Lincoln would leave for the office. He dressed in a plain linen suit. He always wore a tall black hat.

As he walked to the office, he would stop and chat with friends and other lawyers. Everyone called him Lincoln or Mr. Lincoln. Nobody called him Abe. He hated the nickname.

By the time he reached the office, it would be nine o'clock. The firm of Lincoln & Herndon occupied two cluttered rooms on the second floor. Billy Herndon was already at work at his desk by the time Lincoln arrived.

On many cases, the two men worked as a team. Herndon did the research and book work. Lincoln usually appeared in court.

Lincoln could be masterful in front of a jury. He could present a complex matter in easy-to-

The law office of Lincoln & Herndon in Springfield, Illinois.

understand language. He flavored his arguments with humor and amusing stories.

One day Lincoln appeared in court on behalf of a farmer who had been cheated in a horse trade. The lawyer for the other side spoke first. He had his shirt on backward. But no one noticed it except Lincoln.

The lawyer spoke at great length about horses. Then it was Lincoln's turn to speak. "My opponent has been talking about horses for an hour," Lincoln said. "But how much do you think he knows about horses if he doesn't have the sense to put his shirt on right?"

Everyone but the lawyer laughed. Lincoln won the case for the farmer.

For several months each year, Lincoln traveled to circuit courts. He now traveled in a buggy. "Old Buck," his horse, pulled it.

Riding the circuit meant putting up with many hardships. The roads were muddy in winter. They were choked with dust in the summer. The taverns in which he and the other lawyers stayed were often miserable. At night, fleas and bedbugs attacked guests. The tavern food, according to a friend of Lincoln's, "was hardly fit for the stomach of a horse."

But Lincoln didn't mind. He enjoyed life on the circuit. He liked meeting different kinds of people. Most of all, he liked sitting before the fire in the evening, swapping stories with judges and other lawyers.

Lincoln handled hundreds of cases in circuit courts. He became known for his absolute honesty. It was his trademark. He came to be called "Honest Abe."

In notes for a lecture that he wrote about 1850, Lincoln gave advice to those considering a career in law. "Resolve to be honest at all events," he said, "and if, in your own judgment, you can not be an honest lawyer, resolve to be honest without being a lawyer. Choose some other occupation."

Lincoln also appeared in the higher courts. These included the Illinois Supreme Court. He began to represent railroads and big corporations in lawsuits. An Illinois journalist placed Lincoln "at the head of the profession in this state."

During these years, the Lincolns suffered personal tragedy. Late in 1849, the Lincolns' son Eddie, not yet four, fell seriously ill. For almost two months, the Lincolns nursed the child night and day. But their efforts were in vain. Eddie died.

With Eddie's death, Mary Lincoln collapsed in shock. She shut herself in her bedroom and sobbed. She stayed there for weeks.

The Lincolns' third boy arrived on December 21, 1850. He was named William. Lincoln hoped that Willie would make his wife forget Eddie. But nothing could. Years later, Mary would still break down and weep at the mention of Eddie's name.

Late in 1850, Lincoln's father became gravely ill. He died in January 1851.

A fourth son was born to the Lincolns on April 4, 1853. He was named Thomas, after Lincoln's father.

The new baby had a large head and squirmed, said Lincoln, like a tadpole. This caused Lincoln to nickname him "Tad" or "Taddie."

The Lincolns did not believe in disciplining their children. The boys did as they pleased. "It is my pleasure that my children are free and happy, and unrestrained by parental tyranny," Lincoln said.

Billy Herndon knew the Lincoln children as well as anyone. When the partners had to work on Sunday, Lincoln would sometimes bring the boys to the office. They went wild. They pulled books from the shelves. They opened drawers and emptied boxes. They scattered letters and papers over the floor. Then they danced on them.

Lincoln worked away, scarcely noticing what was going on about him. Herndon wanted to grab those "brats" and "wring their necks." But his respect for Lincoln prevented him from doing so.

William Henry Herndon, Lincoln's law partner. This photograph of him dates to about 1871.

These were mostly peaceful days for Lincoln and his family. He was successful in his profession. He was happy in his home.

But in May 1854, Lincoln received news from Washington that upset him. Congress had passed the Kansas-Nebraska Act. The new law said that settlers in the new territories could decide for themselves whether they wanted slavery.

A vast area was affected. It included not only the present states of Kansas and Nebraska, but also the states of North Dakota, South Dakota, Montana, and northern Colorado.

The Kansas-Nebraska Act represented an important change. Slavery had long been banned in the new territories by the Missouri Compromise. The spread of slavery had been held in control. Now slavery had been given new life.

The new law took Lincoln by surprise. He said that he was "thunderstruck and stunned" by it. It was wrong to allow slavery into Kansas and Nebraska, he said. He called the new law a "great moral wrong and injustice."

Lincoln had always been opposed to slavery. He believed that slavery would eventually die out in the South. He looked upon the Southern slave owners as reasonable men. They would free their slaves when it came time for them to do so.

But the Kansas-Nebraska Act upset this view. It could trigger new growth for slavery.

Stephen Douglas, a U.S. senator from Illinois, supported the Kansas-Nebraska Act. He had worked hard in getting the Senate to pass the bill. Lincoln knew Douglas well. In the Illinois State Legislature, Douglas had been leader of the Young Democrats. Lincoln had led the Whigs. The two had often argued about issues.

The people in the territories should be able to decide for themselves whether to keep slaves, Douglas believed. Lincoln represented the opposing point of view. The extension of slavery was wrong, Lincoln declared.

In a speech in Peoria, Illinois, Lincoln explained the evils of the stand that Douglas had taken. It came to be known as "the Peoria Address." It has

Slaves were driven westward as their masters sought new land on the frontier. Many Northerners believed that slavery should not be permitted in the Western territories.

been hailed as the first great speech in Lincoln's career.

"Slavery is founded in the selfishness of man's

nature," Lincoln said in the speech, "opposition to it in his love of justice."

Most Southerners strongly supported Douglas and his efforts to extend slavery into the territories. Northerners were furious. They worked to limit slavery's spread. The anger that developed on both sides helped to bring on the Civil War.

CHAPTER 7

LOSING EFFORT

THE BITTERNESS STIRRED BY THE Kansas-Nebraska Act helped to create a new political party: the Republican party. The Republicans believed slavery to be evil. They opposed the spread of slavery into the Western territories.

The Whig party was falling apart. Its members could not agree upon what to do about slavery.

Many Whigs joined the new Republican party. Abraham Lincoln was one of them.

Late in the spring of 1856, the Republicans nominated John C. Frémont as the party's first presidential candidate.

Lincoln was "a Frémont man." He made more than fifty speeches supporting Frémont. In these, he focused on the slavery question. He called slavery "not only the greatest question, but the sole question of the day."

In the election, the Republicans made a good showing for a new party. But Frémont lost. Democrat James Buchanan became the new president.

In 1857, the year after Frémont's defeat, the Republicans got more bad news. It came in the form of the Dred Scott decision, handed down by the Supreme Court.

Dred Scott had been a slave. He belonged to Dr. John Emerson, an army surgeon. Dr. Emerson took Scott into the territory of Wisconsin and later to Missouri.

Afterward, Scott sued for his freedom. He said that because he had lived in the free territory of Wisconsin and the free state of Missouri he should be declared a free man.

The Supreme Court rejected Scott's claim. The Court declared that slaves were not citizens. Since they were not citizens, they could not sue for their freedom.

Lincoln posed for this picture at a photographer's studio in Chicago on February 28, 1857. He had just passed his forty-eighth birthday. Mrs. Lincoln didn't like the photograph because Lincoln's hair appears uncombed.

The Supreme Court also said that Congress had no right to prohibit slavery in any of the nation's territories.

Republicans were stunned by the Dred Scott decision. They called it "cruel, inhumane, and unfair."

Lincoln read the decision carefully. Then he spoke out against it.

He said that those who had signed the Declaration of Independence had declared that all men, regardless of their skin color, were equal in their right to life, liberty, and the pursuit of happiness. "This they said," Lincoln argued, "and this they meant."

The Dred Scott decision was wrong, Lincoln declared. "We know the court that made it has often overruled its own decisions," he said, "and we will do what we can to have it overrule this."

Lincoln was now looked upon as the leader of the antislavery forces in Illinois. On June 16, 1858, the Republican State Convention chose Lincoln to run for the U.S. Senate. Democrat Stephen Douglas, who was seeking reelection, was to be his opponent.

Lincoln accepted the nomination with a stirring speech. "A house divided against itself cannot stand," Lincoln said. "I believe this government cannot endure, permanently half *slave* and half *free*.

"I do not expect the Union to be *dissolved*—I do not expect the house to fall—but I do expect that it will cease to be divided.

"It will become *all* one thing, or *all* the other."

Lincoln went on to speak of the future of the nation. He said the Republicans must stop the spread of slavery. That wasn't all. They must put slavery back on "the course of ultimate extinction."

In Stephen Douglas, Lincoln had a strong opponent. Douglas was a confident speech maker. His voice boomed out over the audience.

In appearance, Lincoln and Douglas were very different. Douglas was five feet four inches tall. Lincoln was a foot taller. Lincoln's plain suit hung loosely on his lanky frame. Douglas's clothes fitted him neatly.

Douglas opened the campaign in Chicago on July 8, 1858. A huge crowd greeted him.

Douglas declared that Congress had no power to force slavery on the people of a territory. Nor could Congress take slavery away from them. What Congress must do, he said, is "allow the people to decide for themselves whether it is good or evil."

When Lincoln answered Douglas, he branded slavery as a "vast moral evil." He said that it should

Stephen Douglas of Illinois became a member of the U.S. Senate in 1847. He spearheaded passage of the Kansas-Nebraska Act.

be limited to the South so that it could die a natural death.

"Let us unite as one people," he urged, and "once more stand up declaring that all men are created equal."

That summer, Lincoln challenged Douglas to a series of seven debates. Ottawa, in northern Illinois,

People came from miles around to watch Lincoln and Douglas debate during the campaign for the Senate in 1858. This is the scene at Charleston, Illinois, on September 18, as captured by artist Robert Marshall Root. Lincoln is standing. Douglas is seated at his right.

was the scene of the first debate. People by the thousands came from miles around to attend. Flags and banners were hung from buildings. Bands played. Newspapers throughout Illinois carried accounts of the debates. The stories were telegraphed to newspapers in Eastern cities.

The final debate was held in Alton, Illinois, on October 15. Both men were exhausted. Douglas was so hoarse that he was hard to understand. But Lincoln's voice was strong and clear.

On election day, the voting was close. But the Republicans failed to win enough votes to send Lincoln to the Senate. Douglas was the winner.

The defeat hurt Lincoln. He became gloomy. "I feel like the boy who stumped his toe," Lincoln said. "I am too big to cry and too badly hurt to laugh."

THE PEOPLE'S CHOICE

L INCOLN HAD LOST THE ELECTION. But the debates with Stephen Douglas produced an important benefit. They had helped Lincoln to become known in other parts of the country. His name began to be mentioned as a possible candidate in the presidential election of 1860.

Lincoln shrugged off such talk. His ambitions were still focused on the Senate. Stephen Douglas would be seeking reelection in 1864. Lincoln hoped to run against him then.

Early in 1860, Republican leaders launched a Lincoln-for-president campaign. Lincoln did nothing to stop them. He liked the idea of running for president. "The taste *is* in my mouth a little," he would later admit.

In February 1860, Lincoln traveled to New York to make an important speech. It was a chance to impress Republican leaders in the East. Lincoln worked on his speech for weeks. He continued to polish it until the last minute.

About 1,500 people crowded into Cooper Union's Great Hall to hear Lincoln speak. He told the Republicans that they must not weaken on the issue of slavery.

He ended the speech with words that became famous: "Let us have faith that right makes might, and in that faith let us, to the end, dare to do our duty as we understand it."

In other words, Republicans should not be afraid to oppose the extension of slavery. It was the right thing to do. And being right would give them the power to help achieve their goals.

The speech was a hit. It helped to convince Illinois Republicans that Lincoln should run for president.

On his visit to New York in February 1860, the fifty-one-year-old Lincoln posed for this photograph. He appears tall and confident. The pose became known as Lincoln's "Cooper Union" photograph.

That spring, Republicans from every state met in Chicago to choose the party's presidential candidate. New York Senator William Seward had the most support. But on the third ballot, Lincoln edged out Seward and the other hopefuls to win the nomination.

Meanwhile, the Democratic party was splitting apart. Northern Democrats nominated Stephen Douglas as their candidate. Southern Democrats chose John C. Breckenridge of Kentucky. One other party also put forth a candidate.

In the campaign that summer, Republican leaders hailed Lincoln in a thousand and more speeches. Barbecues, parades, and rallies were held on his behalf.

Close to two million Northerners and Westerners turned out to support Lincoln on election day. Their votes swept Lincoln into office.

Hardly had the votes been counted than Lincoln faced a serious problem. Before the election, Southern leaders had urged Southern states to secede—withdraw—from the Union if Lincoln were to win. Lincoln did not take this threat seriously. "The good people of the South," he noted, "had too much good sense and good temper to attempt the ruin of the government."

But the Southern states were more serious than Lincoln judged them to be. South Carolina led the way. In December 1860, South Carolina left the Union.

In January 1861, five other states—Mississippi, Florida, Alabama, Georgia, and Louisiana— followed the lead of South Carolina. The next month, representatives of the six states met in Montgomery, Alabama. There they established the Confederate States of America. Shortly after, Texas joined the Confederacy.

Lincoln had not yet been sworn in as president. Yet already he was facing a severe test.

On a gray February morning in 1861, Lincoln prepared to leave Springfield for Washington for his inauguration. Cold drizzle was falling. Even so, an enormous crowd gathered at the Springfield railroad

In the presidential election of 1860, Hannibal Hamlin, a Senator from Maine, ran as Lincoln's vice president.

depot to say good-bye. Lincoln spoke from the rear platform of his special train. The problems he would soon face were in his thoughts. He said:

To this place and the kindness of these people, I owe every thing. Here I have lived a quarter of a century, and have passed from a young to an old man. Here my children have been born, and one is buried. I now

*leave, not knowing when, or whether ever, I may
return, with a task before me greater than [George
Washington faced]. . . . I bid you affectionate farewell.*

CHAPTER 9

THE WHITE HOUSE AT WAR

On LINCOLN'S FIRST NIGHT AS president, an urgent letter awaited his attention. The letter was from Major Robert Anderson who commanded U.S. troops at Fort Sumter, South Carolina.

Fort Sumter occupied a tiny island at the entrance to Charleston Harbor. The Confederates wanted Sumter. Confederate guns pointed at the fort from shore batteries. Confederate warships stood ready to act.

In his letter, Major Anderson said his supplies would be gone in six weeks.

Lincoln was faced with a tough decision.

Should he seek to hold on to the fort? Or should he order Anderson to abandon it?

Sending a rescue mission to the fort and making a stand was risky. That would surely trigger a civil war.

But letting the Confederates take the fort was no solution. Lincoln had promised to defend federal property that belonged to the United States. If he gave up Sumter, he would be called weak.

Lincoln could not make up his mind. A week went by. Then two weeks. Then a month. Northern newspapers called for Lincoln to *do* something.

At the end of March, Lincoln finally acted. He would not assign more troops to defend Sumter. What he would do is order the navy to send ships carrying supplies to the fort. He would let the Confederates try and stop the ships. If they wanted to fire the first shots of the war, they could do so.

The Confederates learned that the fleet was on the way. They demanded that Major Anderson surrender.

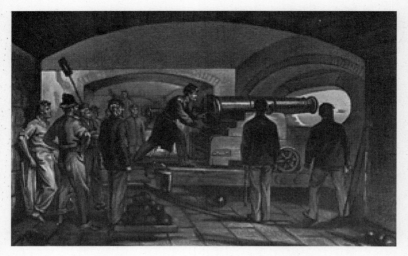

Fort Sumter prepares to answer shelling from Confederate guns.

Anderson refused. On April 12, 1861, Confederate guns opened fire on Fort Sumter.

The first blow had been struck. The Civil War had begun.

Major Anderson and his men answered back with their own guns. But after a day and a half of heavy pounding, they were forced to give up.

Shock and anger swept the North after Fort Sumter's surrender. Lincoln was quick to react. He called for 75,000 volunteers for the army. Then he announced that Union warships would begin stopping all vessels from entering or leaving Southern ports. The blockade was meant to halt trade with Europe.

Once the war began, Virginia, Arkansas, North Carolina, and Tennessee joined the Confederacy. Richmond, Virginia, became the Confederate capital.

As the two sides lined up against one another, the North looked to be stronger than the South. It had many more people. About 22 million citizens lived in the North. About 9 million people lived in the South. But three and one-half million of these Southerners were slaves. At the time the war began, Southerners did not consider using slaves as soldiers.

A bigger population wasn't the North's only advantage. The North had greater industrial strength. It had many hundreds of factories. These could make rifles, cannons, trains, and warships.

The South was devoted mainly to farming. There was little heavy industry.

Many people believed the North could win the war quickly. They called for a major battle that would end the crisis.

Lincoln felt pressured to act. He ordered the Union army to advance from Washington across the Potomac River into Virginia. On July 21, 1861, Union troops met up with Confederate forces near a small creek named Bull Run. The result was a clear victory for the Confederates. Union troops by the hundreds fled back to Washington.

Northerners were shocked. The idea that the war was going to be over quickly ended with the Battle of Bull Run. People now realized that it was going to be a long fight.

Lincoln turned all of his energies toward winning the war. He would be at work at his office by seven o'clock in the morning. He called it his "shop." It was a large room on the second floor of the White House.

From high windows, Lincoln looked out on the south lawn. Beyond was the Washington Monument, which was under construction. Farther to the south

The Lincoln family about 1861, as painted by Francis B. Carpenter. Family members are (from the left): Mrs. Lincoln, Willie, Robert, Tad, and the President.

were the Virginia hills. They were now blanketed with tents erected by the Confederates.

Around nine o'clock, Lincoln would return to the family rooms of the White House. There he would have breakfast with Mary, Tad, and Willie. Young Robert was away at college. Usually Lincoln had an egg and coffee for breakfast.

After he returned to his office, Lincoln studied a digest of the day's news. He also discussed important letters with his two secretaries.

A steady stream of visitors showed up to see Lincoln. Some had favors to ask. Some had complaints. Some simply wanted to shake the president's hand.

At first, Lincoln tried to see everyone. That proved impossible.

His secretaries devised a schedule for him. On Mondays, Wednesdays, and Fridays, the president would see visitors from ten until two. On Tuesdays and Thursdays, he would be available from ten to noon.

But Lincoln often ignored the schedule. He would open the door of his office and let people in whenever he felt like it.

Lunch for Lincoln was often a glass of milk and a biscuit. Afterward, he would return to his office and do paperwork. This included writing important letters. He also sent out short notes to government officials asking them to perform certain duties.

Young Tad and Willie had the run of the White House. Sometimes one or both of them would burst into an office meeting. They played tricks on the White House staff.

The boys collected more than a dozen pets. They rode their pony around the White House grounds. A goat slept in Tad's bed.

They played war. From the White House roof, they would peer out through telescopes, searching for the enemy.

They once planned to "execute" one of their dolls for sleeping while on guard duty. Lincoln came to the doll's rescue. He sent a note to the boys. It read: "The doll Jack is hereby pardoned. By order of the President."

For relaxation, Lincoln would go on carriage rides. Sometimes Mary would go with him.

In the evening, the Lincolns would occasionally attend the theater. Lincoln liked Shakespeare's plays. He also enjoyed opera and concerts.

Usually, however, Lincoln worked late in his office. He sometimes borrowed military textbooks from the Library of Congress. These he studied deep into the night.

In February 1862, the Lincolns' lives were touched again by tragedy. Willie and Tad both came down with a fever. Tad recovered, but the illness took Willie's life. He was eleven years old.

Willie's funeral was held in the East Room of the White House. Lincoln was grief-stricken for weeks.

"My poor boy," said Lincoln. "God called him home. I know that he is much better off in heaven. But then we loved him so. It is hard, hard to have him die."

As the Lincolns sought to mourn their son, the war was expanding. Union forces captured New Orleans in the spring of 1862.

Northern forces also claimed victory at Shiloh in southern Tennessee. But the victory came at a terrible cost. More than 13,000 Union troops were killed or wounded.

Elsewhere, however, there was only bad news. A battle for Richmond in the summer of 1862 ended with the Union army in full retreat.

Confederate forces at the battle for Richmond were commanded by General Robert E. Lee. Again and again, he would prove to be a brilliant leader.

The war was in its second year. Each day brought long lists of dead and wounded to Lincoln's desk. There were times that he wondered whether the war would ever end.

Yet Lincoln seemed to grow stronger and more determined. He believed with all his heart that the Union must be saved. He meant to achieve that goal no matter what the cost.

CHAPTER 10

FREEING THE SLAVES

ABRAHAM LINCOLN WAS OFTEN A patient man. He could put up with long delay. He could wait for the right moment.

It was wrong to force an issue, Lincoln believed. It was better to allow events to unfold naturally.

As an example, Lincoln cited the pear tree. "A man watches his pear tree day after day," Lincoln noted, "impatient for the ripening of the fruit. Let him attempt to *force* the process, and he may spoil both fruit and tree. But let him patiently *wait*, and the ripe pear at length falls into his lap!"

Lincoln had somewhat the same view about

slavery. Early in the war, he felt it was best to let slavery alone in the South. His one goal was to save the Union. Lincoln believed that once the war was won slavery would gradually die out.

"We did not go into the war to put down slavery," he said, "but to put the flag back."

But more and more, Lincoln was being called upon to do something about slavery. Republicans in Congress were among those who wanted him to act. Slavery was the main cause of the war, they said. It was the reason that the Southern states had left the Union. It made no sense to fight a war without destroying the thing that had caused it.

But Lincoln meant to follow his own course. He would not be rushed.

Lincoln's big worry was the "border" states—Delaware, Kentucky, Maryland, and Missouri. These states lay on the border between the North and South. Slavery tied these states to the South.

But they had remained within the Union at the outbreak of the war. Lincoln feared that if he acted now to free the slaves, it would be a mistake. The border states would be angered. They might abandon the North and join the Confederacy.

By the summer of 1862, Lincoln had worked out a plan that would free—or emancipate—the nation's slaves. And it would not upset the border states.

Lincoln told members of his Cabinet what he planned to do. Some opposed the idea. They felt the nation wasn't prepared to accept emancipation. But most Cabinet members favored Lincoln's plan.

On September 22, 1862, Lincoln issued the Emancipation Proclamation. It promised "that on the first day of January, in the year of our Lord, one-thousand, eight-hundred and sixty three, all persons held as slaves" within any of the states of the Confederacy "shall be then, thenceforth and forever free."

The Emancipation Proclamation did not free slaves in rebel territory. They were beyond the reach of federal officers who could enforce it.

Lincoln announced the preliminary Emancipation Proclamation on September 22, 1862. In this engraving, the President is pictured reading the document to his cabinet.

Nor did it apply to slaves within the border states. These states were not "in rebellion" against the United States.

Despite this, the Emancipation Proclamation had an important benefit. It was a symbol. It offered enslaved people the promise of freedom once the Union had won the war.

But Lincoln realized that the Emancipation

Proclamation did not do enough. He called for a constitutional amendment that would "terminate and forever prohibit slavery." The Republicans supported Lincoln's plan.

Lincoln kept pressing the issue. The United States Senate passed the Thirteenth Amendment to the Constitution on April 8, 1864. The House passed it on January 31, 1865. Soon after, it was sent to the states for approval. Lincoln rejoiced.

The Thirteenth Amendment was approved— ratified—by the states on December 18, 1865. The amendment outlawed slavery in every part of America forever.

GETTYSBURG

THE CIVIL WAR HAD RAGED FOR almost two years. Yet victory was nowhere in sight for either side.

Lincoln was deeply troubled. His generals kept disappointing him. He wanted a general who would fight the South harder. He replaced one general after another. But he was unable to find one who satisfied him.

His generals were only one of Lincoln's problems. Manpower was another. The Union army was running out of soldiers. Heavy losses on the battlefield were the chief reason. And thousands of soldiers had deserted their units.

To bring in new recruits, the government decided to draft young men for the army. Those selected in the draft would have to serve.

Lincoln also turned to African Americans. The Emancipation Proclamation did more than grant freedom to slaves. It also stated that African Americans "will be received into the armed service of the United States."

In the spring of 1863, Lincoln urged that large numbers of African Americans be recruited for the Union army. He called the

This young drummer boy was a member of a Union Army infantry unit.

African-American population a "great available... force for restoring the Union."

Most African Americans liked the idea of being able to enlist in the Union army. They crowded into

About 20,000 African-Americans served with the Union navy. Crewmembers aboard the U.S.S. Mendota, a Union gunboat, include several African-American sailors.

recruiting stations in New York, Philadelphia, and Boston.

Eventually, some 180,000 African Americans served with the Union forces. About two-thirds of these were from Southern states. They had fled the South to seek freedom in the North. More than 35,000 African-American servicemen lost their lives in the war.

In the South, it was different. Most people strongly opposed the idea of recruiting slaves to serve with the Confederate army. There was fear that they would turn on their masters.

In the North, Lincoln's policies and programs triggered great discontent. Angry Northerners protested the draft. And many Northerners spoke out against the Emancipation Proclamation. Lincoln made it clear, however, that both were to continue as the law of the land.

As Lincoln sought to cope with citizen unrest, he was brought other disturbing news. General Lee was on the march. His army was heading north. It had pushed across the Maryland border into Pennsylvania.

General Joseph Hooker, in command of the Union army of some 100,000 men, did not try to stop Lee. He said the Confederates outnumbered him. He said he wanted more troops.

Lincoln believed that Hooker was afraid to fight. He replaced him with General George Meade. Meade was sour-faced and had a bad temper. His troops called him "a goggle-eyed old snapping turtle."

The two armies moved through the southern Pennsylvania countryside. They were on a collision course. A great battle loomed.

Near the town of Gettysburg on July 1, Confederate troops ran into Union soldiers. The shooting started. Then fighting got serious and continued through the day. Union troops fell back to occupy a ridge of hills south of the town.

Over the next two days, Lee launched attack after attack on the Union positions. There were heavy losses on both sides.

The climax came on the afternoon of July 3. Lee sent some 15,000 men toward the center of the Union lines. Union soldiers watched as the Southerners advanced in orderly lines. Then Union artillery began pounding away. Union riflemen hit the Southerners with murderous fire. The beaten Confederates fell back. Almost half of the original force lay dead or wounded.

Lee ordered a full retreat. The battle of Gettysburg was over.

This studio photograph of Abraham Lincoln was taken on November 8, 1863, just ten days before he spoke at Gettysburg.

Afterward, Lincoln said that Meade had performed a "great service" at Gettysburg. Indeed, it was true. The Union victory at Gettysburg was a turning point in the war. Lee's crippled army would never again launch a major attack.

Four months later, Lincoln was invited to speak at Gettysburg. A National Soldiers' Cemetery was being dedicated there.

Thousands of people were expected to attend the ceremonies. Edward Everett of Boston was to give the principal address. Everett was one of the greatest speakers of the day.

Lincoln turned down most requests to make speeches. But he accepted the invitation from Gettysburg. He wanted to say something about the meaning of the war.

On November 18, Lincoln took the train to Gettysburg. It was too crowded and noisy on the train to work on his speech. But he went over it that night in the private home where he stayed.

Lincoln finished working on the speech the next morning. Then he joined a procession that marched slowly to the site of the cemetery. Lincoln was dressed in a new black suit. He wore his familiar tall black hat.

The day was filled with sunshine. Some 15,000 people gathered in front of the speaker's platform.

Gettysburg Address

Four score and seven years ago, our fathers brought forth on this continent a new nation, conceived in liberty and dedicated to the proposition that all men are created equal.

Now we are engaged in a great civil war, testing whether that nation or any nation so conceived and so dedicated can long endure. We are met on a great battle field of that war. We have come to dedicate a portion of that field, as a final resting place for those who here gave their lives that this nation might live. It is altogether fitting and proper that we should do this.

But, in a larger sense, we can not dedicate—we can not consecrate—we can not hallow—this ground. The brave men, living and dead, who struggled here, have consecrated it, far above our poor power to add or detract. The world will little note, nor long remember, what we say here, but it can never forget what they did here. It is for us the living, rather, to be here dedicated to the unfinished work which they who fought here have thus far so nobly advanced. It is rather for us to be here dedicated to the great task remaining before us—that from these honored dead we take increased devotion to that cause for which they gave the last full measure of devotion—that we here highly resolve that these dead shall not have died in vain—that this nation, under God, shall have a new birth of freedom—and that government of the people, by the people, for the people, shall not perish from the earth.

The speakers could see wood coffins in the open fields awaiting burial.

Edward Everett spoke first. He described the three-day battle that had taken place at Gettysburg only months before. He spoke for two hours.

Then it was Lincoln's turn. The president took his two-page speech from his coat pocket and stepped to the front of the platform. "Four score and seven years ago," he began, "our fathers brought forth on this continent a new nation..."

Lincoln spoke for about two minutes. Few expected so brief an address. As he sat down, the audience applauded politely.

Afterward, Lincoln had doubts whether the speech was successful. He remarked to a friend that "it fell upon the audience like a wet blanket."

Most newspapers gave much more space to Edward Everett's speech than to Lincoln's. But some had warm praise for what the president had to say. *The Washington Chronicle* declared that the president's speech, "though short, glittered with gems." Said

Harper's Weekly: "The few words of the President were from the heart to heart."

People everywhere recognized the speech for its power. The war was about more than the Union, Lincoln said. He spoke of equality. He spoke of human freedom.

In time, of course, Lincoln's speech at Gettysburg came to be hailed as one of the greatest speeches in history. It is reprinted on postcards and in history textbooks. It is available in pamphlets.

It appears on the side wall of the Lincoln Memorial in Washington, D.C. More than twenty books have been written about the Gettysburg Address.

Grade school students memorize it. Thousands of Americans know it word for word. The words of the Gettysburg Address are as powerful today as they were over a hundred years ago.

CHAPTER 12

"WITH CHARITY FOR ALL"

"I LIKE THAT MAN. HE FIGHTS." LINCOLN used these words to describe General Ulysses S. Grant. Early in 1864, the president named the forty-two-year-old Grant to head the Union armies.

It was not a hard choice to make. Grant had scored a string of battlefield victories.

Grant was born in Port Pleasant, Ohio. At West Point, he became a skilled horseman. After graduation, Grant served as a captain in the Mexican War. He left the army in 1854. But when Lincoln called for volunteers in 1861, Grant signed up again.

Lincoln and Grant mapped out a grand plan to

General Ulysses S. Grant at his headquarters at Cold Harbor, Virginia. This photograph was taken on June 11 or 12, 1864, about three months after Grant had been named head of the Union armies by Lincoln.

smash General Lee and the Southern armies. They would attack on all fronts. They would launch "total war."

The strategy soon began to produce results. Grant himself led an attack against Lee's troops in Virginia. At the same time, General William T. Sherman struck at the Confederates. Sherman's army advanced through Tennessee and Georgia toward Atlanta.

As the war raged on, Lincoln began to think about the presidential election to be held in November. The president wanted a second term in office. He truly believed, as he said, that he could "better serve the nation in its need and peril than any new man could possibly do."

In addition, being reelected would be a stamp of approval. It would mean that the nation's voters supported the Union cause. It would also mean that they supported the Emancipation Proclamation.

In June 1864, Lincoln was chosen for a second term by the National Union Convention. The Convention was made up of not only Republicans, but also "pro-Union" Democrats. Andrew Johnson of Tennessee was chosen to run as Lincoln's vice president.

To oppose Lincoln, the Democrats decided upon George B. McClellan. This was the same McClellan that had failed Lincoln as commander of the Union army.

When Lincoln sought reelection in 1864, Andrew Johnson, a former Tennessee senator, ran as his vice president.

McClellan promised to bring peace "at the earliest possible moment." He also said he would restore the Union and permit slavery.

Lincoln worried that he might lose the election to McClellan. Support for the war was fading. Grant was pressing the enemy hard, but his tactics had cost the lives of many thousands of soldiers.

Lincoln was deeply affected by the bloodshed. A White House visitor found that the president was unable to sleep, "pacing back and forth ... with great black rings under his eyes."

The news from General Grant was not good. Grant had attacked Petersburg, Virginia. From there, he planned to move on to Richmond. But Grant was unable to take Petersburg. He dug in and prepared for months of fighting.

During the summer of 1864, the battlefield situation began to change for the Union. Victories replaced defeats. Admiral David G. Farragut won the Battle of Mobile (Alabama) Bay. General Sherman's troops captured Atlanta, the Queen City of the South.

The victories encouraged Northerners. They felt more confident about Lincoln. In the election that fall, Lincoln defeated McClellan by almost half a million votes.

Lincoln was fifty-five now. He looked older. The war had taken a heavy toll on him.

Mary Lincoln was worried about her husband. She said that he seemed "so broken hearted, so completely worn out."

March 4, 1865, was Inauguration Day. Lincoln took his place on the special platform that had been

On March 4, 1865, Lincoln took the oath of office for the second time.

built in front of the Capitol. There he took his oath of office a second time.

His inauguration speech was like his address at Gettysburg. It was not long. It did not waste words. It was forceful and very moving.

The time had come, Lincoln said, for healing, for mercy.

He ended the address with these words:

With malice toward none; with charity for all; with firmness in the right, as God gives us to see the right, let us strive on to finish the work we are in; to bind up the nation's wounds, to care for him who shall have borne the battle, and for his widow, and his orphan— to do all which may achieve and cherish a just, and a lasting peace among ourselves, and with all nations.

As Lincoln spoke, the end of the war was clearly in sight. After Atlanta, Sherman had marched southeast through Georgia to the coastal city of Savannah. On its way, Sherman's army destroyed everything in its path.

From Savannah, Sherman pressed north into South Carolina. On February 7, he marched into Charleston, the capital.

Sherman kept moving. After Charleston, he advanced into North Carolina and Virginia. His plan was to link his army with Grant's.

Conditions in the South had become desperate. There were shortages of food and supplies. The terrible loss of life had cast widespread sadness and gloom.

Late in March 1865, General Grant invited Lincoln to visit him at his headquarters at City Point, Virginia, east of Petersburg. Lincoln accepted the invitation. He decided to bring his wife and Tad with him.

Mary Lincoln was happy to be leaving Washington. She believed that Washington was filled with enemies. City Point would be safer. Besides, the rest and fresh air would be good for the president.

On March 23, the Lincolns boarded the *River Queen*. The steamer sailed down the Potomac River into Chesapeake Bay, then headed south.

At City Point, Lincoln met with Grant and his generals. They talked about the end of the war, which was drawing near.

While at City Point, Lincoln was brought the news that Grant's troops had cracked the Confederate defenses at Petersburg and swept into the city. Soon after, the Union army marched into Richmond. Leaders of the Confederate government fled the city.

Lincoln wanted to visit Richmond. He was curious to see the now battered city, which had been the symbol of the Confederacy.

On April 4, Lincoln, along with Tad, sailed the short distance up the James River from City Point to Richmond. Some buildings were still burning as Lincoln and his son stepped ashore. Thick black smoke hung over the city.

Black slaves, who were now free, recognized the president. They clustered about him, cheering and laughing.

The president took Tad's hand and walked up Richmond's Main Street. Six sailors armed with rifles walked ahead of them.

Throughout the day, hundreds of people flocked around the president. He was watched from every window.

Members of Grant's staff who were with the president worried about his safety. It was almost impossible to protect him as he walked through the crowded streets.

At one point, a man in a Confederate soldier's

After the Union army had taken Richmond, Lincoln visited the city. Cheering crowds greeted him as he walked the city's streets with his son Tad.

uniform was spotted at a window. He appeared to point a rifle at Lincoln. But no shot was fired.

The next morning, Lincoln was warned that he was in great danger. He was advised to be more careful if he went ashore again. But Lincoln did not take the warning seriously. He said, "I cannot bring myself to believe that any human being lives who would do me any harm."

CHAPTER 13

"I KNOW I'M IN DANGER..."

THE STEAMER *RIVER QUEEN* CARRYING President Lincoln arrived back in Washington on April 9, 1865. Edwin Stanton, Lincoln's Secretary of War, was waiting on the dock.

Stanton had the news that Lincoln had been praying for. General Lee had surrendered. Lee had met General Grant at a place called Appomattox Courthouse in Virginia, and agreed to lay down his guns.

Lincoln was overjoyed. The president and Stanton threw their arms around one another.

The long war was over. It had lasted four years

and had taken a heavy toll. About 620,000 soldiers died during the war. That is about equal to the total number of Americans that died in all other American wars.

With the war's end, Washington celebrated. People laughed and cheered. Hundreds of cannons boomed. Bells rang out

Lincoln, meanwhile, was worried about the helpless South. Many Northern political leaders wanted to punish Confederate leaders. Lincoln took a softer approach. He wanted to help rebuild and restore the South. He also wanted to protect the rights of the freed slaves.

Although peace had come, those close to the president were still deeply concerned about his safety. They feared that someone who had supported the Confederate cause might try to kidnap or kill him. Hardly a day went by that Lincoln did not receive a threatening letter.

Lincoln shrugged off the idea that he might be someone's target. He said, "I long ago made up my

Taken on February 5, 1865, this is the final studio portrait made of Lincoln. The pressure of war showed in the president's face. A friend noted that he looked "haggard with care . . . weatherbeaten." Less than seven weeks after the picture was taken, Lincoln was assassinated.

mind that if anyone wants to kill me, he will do it. I know I'm in danger but I'm not going to worry about it."

Lincoln's advisers, however, took steps to protect

him. The president was assigned personal bodyguards. When Lincoln took his afternoon carriage ride, mounted troops rode along to protect him.

April 14, 1865, a Friday, began as a normal day for the president. He began work at seven o'clock. Routine tasks occupied him.

At breakfast, Robert joined his parents. As a member of General Grant's staff, Robert had been at Appomattox Courthouse, Virginia, when Lee had surrendered to Grant. He reported details of the historic meeting to his father and mother.

Later, back at the office, Lincoln met with visitors. At 11 o'clock, there was a Cabinet meeting.

Lincoln was too busy that day for lunch. He ate an apple. In the afternoon, there were papers to sign and more people to see.

At three o'clock, the president and his wife went for a carriage ride. Their journey took them to the navy yard, in the southeastern part of the city. Lincoln went aboard the *Montauk*, a Union warship. He chatted with several sailors.

Throughout the afternoon, Lincoln was in high spirits. "Dear Husband," Mary said to him, "you almost startle me with your great cheerfulness."

Back at the White House, there were more visitors to see. But Lincoln broke away from his office tasks for an early dinner. He and Mary were planning to go to Ford's Theatre that evening. They were to see a play titled *Our American Cousin*. It was a popular comedy of the day.

Stanton and several other of Lincoln's advisers warned Lincoln not to go to the theater that night. Stanton worried that some crazed person might take a shot at Lincoln from the street. But Lincoln stuck to his plans.

The Lincolns' carriage was late getting to the theater. The play had already started. When Lincoln and his wife appeared in their box seats, the audience stood and cheered and applauded. The orchestra saluted Lincoln by playing "Hail to the Chief." The president smiled and bowed.

The play resumed. Lincoln sat back and relaxed. Mary sat next to him. Henry R. Rathbone, a young army major, and Clara Harris, to whom he was engaged, were the guests of the Lincolns that night. They were seated in the box with the Lincolns.

Behind the president and Mrs. Lincoln and their guests, the door to their box was closed. But it was not locked. Nor was it guarded. Lincoln's bodyguard that evening, John Parker, had left his post.

The Lincolns appeared to enjoy the play. Mary applauded. Lincoln laughed heartily. At one point, Lincoln felt a chill. He got up and put on his overcoat.

Onstage, the actors recited their lines. One of the lines caused the audience to burst into roaring laughter.

At this point, the door behind the president swung open. A man with a pistol slipped into the presidential box. Then he placed the pistol close to the back of the president's head and fired. Lincoln slumped forward. Mary threw her arms around her husband. Then she screamed.

Major Rathbone lunged at the gunman. He yelled something and lashed out at Rathbone with a knife.

Rathbone felt a sting of pain. The gunman had cut Rathbone's arm.

The attacker leaped from the box to the stage. In leaping, he caught a spur of his boot in a flag draped over the front of the box. He went crashing to the stage. In the fall, he broke a bone in his leg.

Limping across the stage, he stopped and shouted, *Sic semper tyrannis* (which is Latin for "Thus it shall ever be for tyrants"). Then he hobbled offstage. In the alley at the back of the theater, a boy held a horse for him. The gunman mounted the horse and galloped off into the night.

The audience was stunned. No one was sure what had happened. Someone shouted out "Booth!" Then others in the audience began to call out the name "Booth! Booth! Booth!"

They had recognized the man who had leaped from the box. It was John Wilkes Booth. He was a noted actor of the day. Booth supported the Confederacy. He approved of slavery. He believed that Lincoln was responsible for the war.

"Stop that man! Stop that man! Won't somebody

stop that man?" screamed Clara Harris. "The president is shot!"

The unconscious Lincoln was carried from the theater. He was brought across the street to the bedroom of a narrow, three-story house. The bed on which he was placed was too short for his tall frame. Lincoln had to be slanted across the mattress.

The small bedroom was crowded with

John Wilkes Booth was the president's assassin. Born in Maryland, he was a well-known actor of the time.

people. When Mary Lincoln arrived, she threw herself across Lincoln, sobbing. A friend of Mary's convinced her to rest in the parlor. There Mary would spend most of the night.

Several doctors were at the president's bedside. They agreed that Lincoln had no chance to recover.

The president never regained consciousness. He died at 7:22 on the morning of April 15.

Lincoln's funeral was held in the East Room of the White House. Mrs. Lincoln, deep in grief, was unable to attend the services. She stayed upstairs.

Afterward, a long procession bore Lincoln's coffin to the Capitol. The next day, thousands filed past the open coffin to pay their last respects to Lincoln.

On Friday, April 21, just a week after Lincoln had been shot, his body left Washington in a nine-car funeral train. Earlier, Willie Lincoln's coffin had been taken from its grave and put in the funeral car.

The funeral train was bound for Springfield. There Lincoln and his son would be buried.

The train stopped at major cities along the 1,600-mile route. At each stop, mourners were given a chance to file past the open coffin.

In New York City, 85,000 people took part in a

Thousands watch as Lincoln's funeral procession makes its way up Broadway in New York City.

procession that escorted Lincoln's coffin through the streets.

From New York City, the funeral train traveled to Albany and Buffalo. As the train headed west across Ohio, news was received that Union soldiers had hunted down John Wilkes Booth. He had been shot and killed in a tobacco barn near Port Royal, Virginia.

Others who were said to have joined forces with Booth in an earlier plot to kidnap the president had also been arrested. Four of these people were eventually convicted and hung.

When the funeral train arrived in Springfield, tens of thousands of people were waiting to meet it. "There was an overpowering feeling of loss," Philip B. Kunhardt, Jr., declared in *Lincoln, An Illustrated Biography*. "People had to keep a grip on themselves when the realization came over them...that they would never see Abraham Lincoln again."

LINCOLN
REMEMBERED

ABRAHAM LINCOLN WAS THE FIRST American president to be shot to death. His murder sent shock waves through the nation. A great outpouring of grief followed.

Houses, shops, and buildings were decorated with black ribbon or other signs of mourning. People hung memorial portraits of Lincoln in their homes. They pinned on mourning ribbons. Some wore pins or badges bearing Lincoln's portrait.

Many hundreds of monuments and memorials would be erected in Lincoln's honor. One of the most important is the Lincoln National

*After Lincoln's death, artists often pictured him with George
Washington. Washington had been named the "father of our
country." Lincoln was called the nation's "savior."*

Monument. A towering shaft of granite, it was
dedicated in Springfield, Illinois, in 1874.

Before it stands a bronze figure of Lincoln. The
Lincoln National Monument is the final resting
place of the Lincoln family.

The Lincoln Memorial in Washington, D.C., was

dedicated on May 30, 1922. It stands at the west end of National Mall.

It takes the form of an enormous white marble temple. Thirty-six massive columns surround it. Within the structure is a huge marble statue of a seated Lincoln. The memorial is an awesome tribute to the sixteenth president.

Thirty-four American cities have been named after Lincoln. These include Lincoln, Nebraska, the capital of the state. Twenty-two of the nation's counties honor his name.

Within months after Lincoln's death, written accounts of his life began to appear. The stream of books has continued to this day. More books have been written about Lincoln than any other American. Countless movies and plays have featured Lincoln.

In 1909, the hundredth anniversary of Lincoln's birth, the Lincoln cent was issued. It was the first American coin to bear a president's image. Billions are minted each year.

When first issued, the coin drew some complaints.

This sculpted image of Lincoln by Victor D. Brenner was used in designing the Lincoln cent.

Some people said that Lincoln deserved to be honored with a more important coin than the penny. But others praised the coin. They argued that Lincoln was "the people's president." The penny, therefore, was quite proper.

Lincoln's portrait also appears on the five-dollar bill. The first five-dollar bills with Lincoln's image were issued in 1924.

Earlier, Lincoln's image appeared on the one hundred-dollar-bill. These bills were first issued in 1869.

Lincoln's portrait also appears on postage stamps, medals, and tokens.

Lincoln's name has come to indicate honesty. It has been used by many savings banks. Insurance companies also use Lincoln's name.

Many national historic sites have been established in Lincoln's honor. These include his birthplace, his boyhood home, and the home in which he and his family lived.

Presidents' Day, the third Monday in February, is a legal holiday in the United States that honors both Abraham Lincoln and George Washington. Lincoln's birthday, February 12, is a legal holiday in about thirty states.

Lincoln's life ended suddenly that night at Ford's Theatre. But his words and his deeds are certain to be remembered for as long as the nation exists.

CHRONOLOGY

1809   (February 12) Lincoln is born.

1832   Serves as volunteer in Black Hawk's War.

1834   Elected to Illinois State Legislature.

1836   Receives license as lawyer.

1842   (November 4) Marries Mary Todd.

1846   Elected to U.S. House of Representatives.

1858   In election for U.S. Senate, is defeated by Senator Stephen A. Douglas.

1860   (May 18) Wins Republican presidential nomination.

1860   (November 6) Elected President of the United States.

1861   (March 4) Inaugurated as sixteenth United States president.

1861   (April 12) Civil War begins.

1863   (January 1) Issues final Emancipation Proclamation.

1863   (November 19) Delivers Gettysburg Address.

1864   (November 8) Reelected president.

1865   (April 9) Civil War ends.

1865   (April 14) Shot by John Wilkes Booth.

1865   (April 15) Dies in Washington, D.C.

1865   (May 4) Buried in Springfield, Illinois.

BIBLIOGRAPHY

Primary Sources

An Oral History of Abraham Lincoln: John G. Nicolay's Interviews
and Essays. Carbondale, Illinois: University of Illinois Press,
1994.

Ayres, Alex, editor. *The Wit and Wisdom of Abraham Lincoln.*
New York: Meridian, 1992.

Basler, Roy P., editor, *The Collected Works of Abraham Lincoln.*
New Brunswick, New Jersey: Rutgers University Press, 1955.

Fehrenbacher, Don E., editor. *Abraham Lincoln, A Documentary
Portrait Through His Speeches and Writings.* Stanford,
California: Stanford University Press, 1964.

Lincoln, Abraham. *Speeches and Writings: 1859–1865.* New
York: Library of America, 1959.

Williams, T. Harry, editor. *Selected Writings and Speeches of
Abraham Lincoln.* Hendricks House, 1980.

Secondary Sources

Bishop, Jim. *The Day Lincoln Was Shot.* New York: Harper &
Row, 1955.

Braden, Waldo W. *Abraham Lincoln, Public Speaker.* Baton
Rouge, Louisiana: Louisiana State University Press, 1988.

Donald, David Herbert. *Lincoln.* New York: Touchstone, 1995.

Kunhardt, Dorothy Meserve and Philip B. Kunhardt, Jr. *Twenty
Days.* New York: Harper & Row, 1965.

Miers, Earl Schenk, editor in chief. *Lincoln Day by Day. A
Chronology, 1869–1865* (3 vols.). Washington: Lincoln
Sesquicentennial Commission, 1960.

Neely, Mark E., Jr. *The Abraham Lincoln Encyclopedia.* New York:
McGraw Hill, 1982.

Oates, Stephen B. *With Malice Toward None, A Life of Abraham Lincoln*. New York: HarperCollins, 1994.

Ostendorf, Lloyd. *Lincoln's Photographs, A Complete Album*. Dayton, Ohio: Rockywood Press, 1998.

Sandburg, Carl. *Abraham Lincoln: The Prairie Years* (2 vols.). New York: Harcourt, Brace, 1926.

_____ *Abe Lincoln Grows Up*. New York: Harcourt, Brace, 1929.

_____ *Abraham Lincoln: The War Years* (4 vols.). Harcourt, Brace, 1939.

FURTHER READING

Bial, Raymond. *Where Lincoln Walked*. New York: Walker, 1997.

Freedman, Russell. *Lincoln: A Photobiography*. New York: Clarion Books, 1987.

Lincoln, Abraham. *The Gettysburg Address*. Illustrated by Michael McCurdy. Boston: Houghton Mifflin, 1995.

Meltzer, Milton, editor. *Lincoln in His Own Words*. San Diego: Harcourt Brace, 1993.

North, Sterling. *Abe Lincoln, Log Cabin to White House*. New York: Random House, 1956.

FOR MORE INFORMATION

Abraham Lincoln Birthplace National Historical Site
Hodgenville, Kentucky
Write for brochure containing information about Abraham
Lincoln, the Hodgenville area, and his birthplace site.
(2995 Lincoln Farm Rd., Hodgenville, KY 42748)
Phone: (517) 358-3117
Web site: www.nps.gov/abli/

Ford's Theatre
Washington, D.C.
Makes available a colorful brochure called *Ford's Theatre and
The House Where Lincoln Died.* It describes events surrounding the
assassination. Request a copy.
(Ford's Theatre, National Park Service, 517 10th St. NW,
Washington, D.C. 20004)
Phone: (202) 426-6924
Web site: www.nps.gov/foth

Lincoln Boyhood National Memorial
Lincoln City, Indiana
Provides background information on the southern Indiana farm
country where Lincoln spent his formative years.
(P. O. Box 1816, Lincoln City, IN 47552)
Phone: (812) 937-4541
Web site: www.nps.gov/libo/index/htm

Lincoln Home National Historic Site
Springfield, Illinois
Write for a brochure describing the only home that Lincoln ever owned and where he and his family lived for seventeen years.
(426 South Seventh St., Springfield, IL 62701)
Phone: (217) 492-4241
Web site: www.nps.gov/liho

Springfield Visitors Bureau
Springfield, Illinois
Makes available a Family Vacation Planning Kit with information about historic sites related to Lincoln in Springfield.
(109 North Seventh St., Springfield, IL 62701)
Phone: (800) 545-7310
Web site: www.springfield.il.us/visit

PHOTO CREDITS

Library of Congress: 6, 35, 40, 42, 47, 66, 76, 84, 91, 97, 105, 108, 120; George Sullivan: 11, 73, 88, 99, 113; Lloyd Ostendorf: 13, 58; New York Public Library: 16, 20, 44, 54, 61, 69, 101, 115; Illinois State Historical Library: 23, 28, 32, 62; Lincoln Home National Historic Site: 37; Lloyd Ostendorf/Ingmire: 51; National Archives: 87; The Lincoln Museum: 118.

INDEX

Bold numbers refer to photographs